· CREATIVE CRAFTS ·

MAKING
PRESENTS

· JULIET BAWDEN ·

NOTE TO PARENTS

For some of the presents in this book, an oven, varnish, a sharp knife, or scissors may be needed. Please note which projects will require your supervision and talk to your children about safety.

Before starting a project, you may want to cover the work space with sheets of newspaper or a plastic cloth, to make cleaning up easier. For messy projects, you may also want children to wear an apron or old shirt to protect their clothing.

ACKNOWLEDGMENTS

Presents made by Karen Radford,
Ann Marie Mulligan, and Anne Sharples
Photographs by David Johnson
Illustrations by Elizabeth Kerr

HAMLYN CHILDREN'S BOOKS
Series Editor : Anne Civardi
Series Designer : Anne Sharples
Production Controller : Linda Spillane

First American edition, 1994

Library of Congress Cataloging-in-Publication Data
Bawden, Juliet.
Making presents / Juliet Bawden.
p.   cm. — (Creative crafts)
Summary: Includes instructions and "handy hints" for making all kinds of gifts, such as clay buttons, picture frames, magnets, bows, and paper pots.
ISBN 0-679-83495-8 (trade) — ISBN 0-679-93495-2 (lib. bdg)
1. Handicraft — Juvenile literature. [1. Handicraft. 2. Gifts.]
I. Title. II. Series: Creative crafts (New York, N.Y.)
TT160.B335 1993
745.5—dc20   92–18649

Manufactured in Belgium

10 9 8 7 6 5 4 3 2 1

CONTENTS

MATERIALS, TIPS, AND HINTS

In this book there are all sorts of easy but exciting presents for you to make. There are presents for babies, brothers and sisters, friends, moms, dads, and grandparents.

You can probably find most of the things you need to make them with around the house, but you may need to buy a few special things.

Before you start making a present, read the instructions carefully to find out what you need. The Handy Hints give you lots of extra ideas and help you make the presents.

Things to collect

Cardboard boxes and plastic
  containers (like those for
  yogurt or margarine)
Cardboard tubes (like those for
  paper towels) and egg cartons
Cardboard — such as empty
  cereal boxes and the backs of
  notepads
Paper — old newspapers,
  scraps of colored paper, used
  stamps, drawing paper, old
  magazines, old wrapping
  paper, birthday cards, and old
  postcards
Used lollipop sticks, ice cream
  sticks, garden markers, or thin
  straight sticks
String, ribbon, wool, corks,
  tinfoil, toothpaste or tomato
  paste tubes, Plasticine, bag
  ties, paper clips, buttons, and
  beads

Useful tips

1. You will need poster paints or tempera paints for some of the presents you make. Ready-mixed poster paints are sold in jars. For a few projects you will need acrylic or enamel paints.

Before you varnish a present, make sure you have the right varnish. Use water-based varnish unless otherwise specified.

Put tops back on tightly to keep paints and glue from drying out.

Wash your paintbrushes well after you have used them and store them with the bristles facing upward. Use turpentine to remove oil-based varnish and enamel paints.

Keep modeling materials, such as self-hardening clay or salt dough, in plastic bags to keep them from drying. Keep salt dough in the refrigerator.

You can make presents with more than one material. For example, instead of salt dough you could use self-hardening clay or papier-mâché.

2. There are different brands of self-hardening clay. Read the instructions on the package very carefully to see how long they take to harden in the oven. Some do not need to be baked at all.

3. You can make papier-mâché with wallpaper paste, following the instructions on the package. Or you can just use flour and water (see page 9 for the recipe).

4. To make many of the presents you need glue. Glue sticks are clean and easy to use. Strong glue works best on rubber, cardboard, and paper. Use a fabric glue for fabrics.

NIFTY NAME PLATES

You can make these fancy name plates very easily out of salt, flour, and water. Here are lots of ideas on how to decorate and paint them, and the different shapes and sizes you can make.

Things you need

1½ cups salt, 1½ cups flour, and 1 tbs. oil
½ cup water, baking tray and wax paper
Tempera or poster paints, paintbrushes
Clear varnish and paper clips

Nifty name plate

Making the dough

1. Preheat oven to 350°F. Mix the salt, flour, and oil together in a bowl. Mix in the water, a little at a time, until you have a big ball of dough.

2. Put the dough on a floured surface and knead it with your hands until it is very smooth and elastic. If it is too dry, add a little more water.

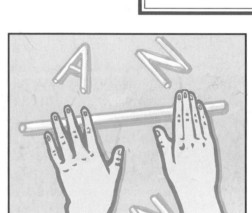

1. Draw the shape of your name plate on wax paper. Sprinkle the paper with flour and then press a lump of dough onto the paper to fill the shape.

2. To make the letters on your name plate, roll dough into thin sausage shapes. Form each of the sausage shapes into a letter of your name.

3. Carefully press the letters onto your name plate (use a little water to help the dough stick) and add decorations. Push a paper clip into the top, as shown.

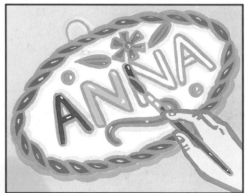

4. Put the name plate and wax paper on a baking tray and bake it in the middle of the oven until it is hard. This should take about an hour.

5. Take the name plate out of the oven and wait until it is completely cool. Then paint it with bright tempera or poster paints. Let the paint dry.

6. Varnish the name plate on the front and let it dry. Then varnish the back. When it is dry, apply another coat of varnish to each side. Let it dry.

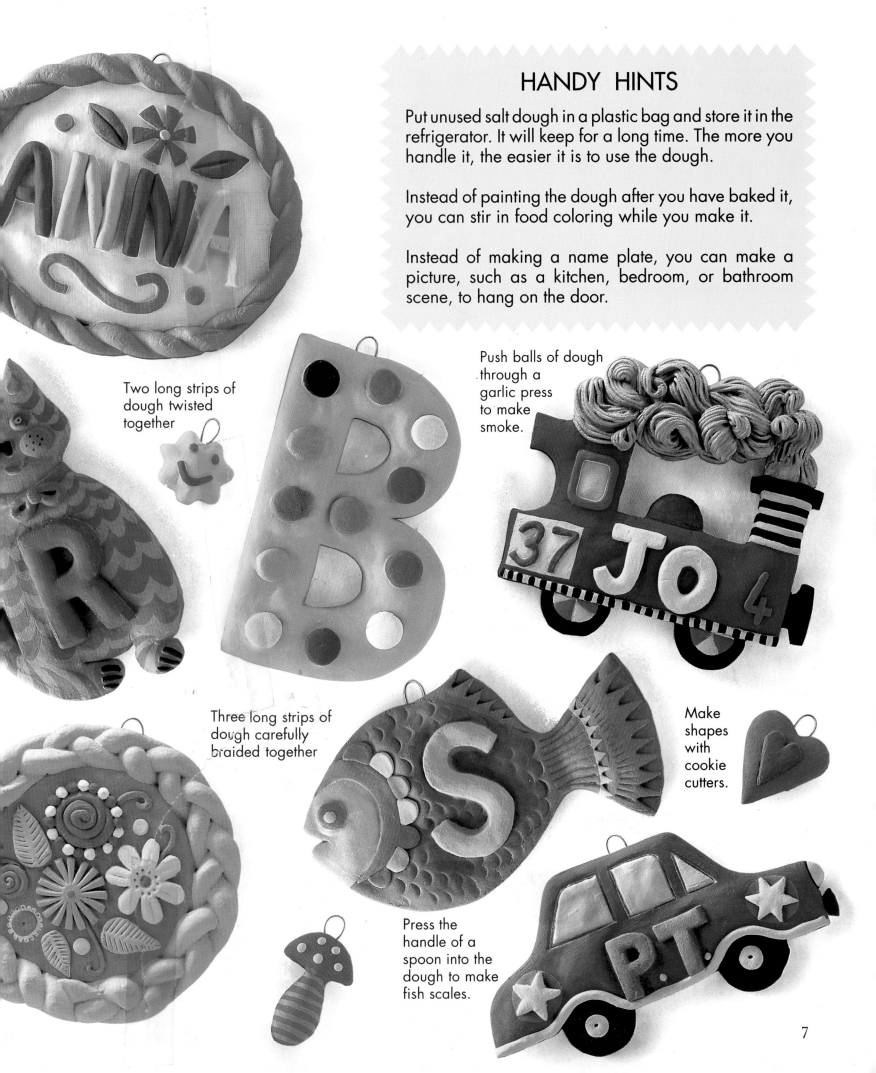

Put unused salt dough in a plastic bag and store it in the refrigerator. It will keep for a long time. The more you handle it, the easier it is to use the dough.

Instead of painting the dough after you have baked it, you can stir in food coloring while you make it.

Instead of making a name plate, you can make a picture, such as a kitchen, bedroom, or bathroom scene, to hang on the door.

Two long strips of dough twisted together

Push balls of dough through a garlic press to make smoke.

Three long strips of dough carefully braided together

Make shapes with cookie cutters.

Press the handle of a spoon into the dough to make fish scales.

7

PERKY PIGGY BANKS

For a very useful present, you can make a special piggy bank. These are made out of papier-mâché (layers of newspaper and glue) shaped around balloons. You can use different shaped balloons to make various animals, such as a pig, crocodile, or fish. They will take a couple of days to make as each layer of papier-mâché takes a while to dry.

Things you need

Small round balloon
Newspaper
Wallpaper paste
Five corks
Masking tape
Strips of thin cardboard
Scissors
Thin wire (a garbage bag tie is ideal)
Tempera or poster paints
Paintbrush

Perky
pink
pig

Pink pig piggy bank

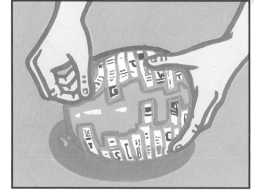

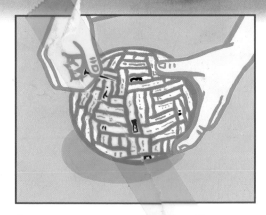

1. Blow up the balloon to the size you want the pig to be. Tie a knot in it. Mix the wallpaper paste, following the instructions on the package. Then tear sheets of newspaper into strips about 1 in. wide and 4 in. long.

2. Cover a strip of paper with paste, wiping off the extra paste between your thumb and first finger. Stick the paper onto the balloon. Do the same with more strips of paper until the balloon is covered. Let dry.

3. Stick six layers of paper onto the balloon, letting each one dry before adding the next. When they are all dry, carefully stick a pin through the papier-mâché shell so that you pop the balloon inside.

Fantastic fish
money box

HANDY HINTS

You can make your own paste from one cup of flour and three cups of water.

Mix the flour with a little of the water in a saucepan, stirring until it becomes a smooth paste. Add the rest of the water and stir.

Ask a grownup to heat the mixture until it boils, stirring all the time. Simmer until the paste thickens. Let the mixture cool.

Paint your bank with clear varnish to give it a hard, strong finish.

Shape this crazy
crocodile around
a long, thin balloon.
Add a cardboard nose
and tail, and cork feet.

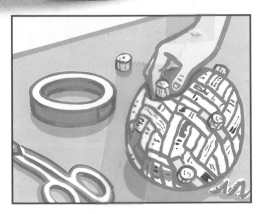

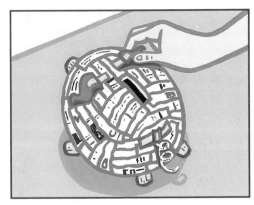

4. Cut one cork in half and tape it onto the papier-mâché shell to make the pig's nose. Tape on the other four corks to make the legs. Shape the wire into a curly tail and cover it with papier-mâché. Tape it onto the body.

5. Cut out two cardboard ears and tape them onto the pig's head. Now stick two more layers of papier-mâché over the pig's body, legs, nose, and ears. Cut a slit in the top to drop the money through.

6. When the pig is completely dry, you can paint it with tempera or poster paints. Brush on a base color first and then let it dry. Decorate the pig and paint on eyes, nostrils, and a mouth.

BRIGHT BUTTONS

Make your own animal, flower, heart, and alphabet buttons out of brightly colored self-hardening clay or painted salt dough. You can sew them onto thick paper and turn them into special birthday and thank-you cards or invitations. Create unusual pictures for presents, too!

Things you need

Self-hardening clay in bright colors
Tracing paper and pencil
Scissors
Thick paper or cardboard
Felt tip pens
Needle and thread
Baking tray and knife
Clear varnish or clear nail polish

Special card for
Valentine's Day

Small number
buttons to sew
on a cardigan

10

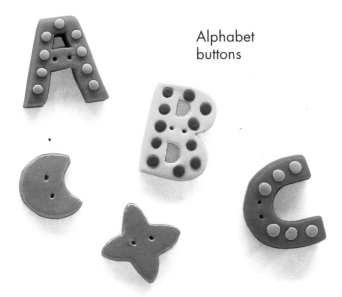

Alphabet buttons

HANDY HINTS

If you do not have any self-hardening clay, make the buttons out of salt dough (see page 6 for the recipe). Paint and varnish the dough buttons when you have baked them.

Instead of making a tracing paper shape to cut around, use tiny cookie cutters in different shapes to make your buttons.

Make a special set of buttons for one of your friends to sew on a cardigan.

Froggy button picture

1. Draw a funny frog's face on a sheet of tracing paper, as shown. Cut out the paper frog shape and use it as a pattern.

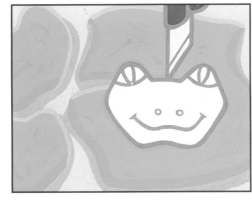

2. Roll out green self-hardening clay, about as thick as a button. Put the frog shape on the clay and cut around it with a knife. Cut out three frog faces.

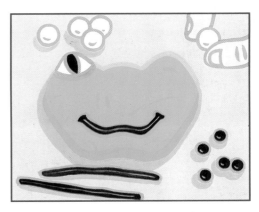

3. Roll out six little white balls of clay and six smaller black balls for the frogs' eyes. Press them onto the three faces, as shown. Press on smiley black mouths.

4. Make two holes in the middle with a needle. Put the buttons on a baking tray. Bake them according to the instructions on the package.

5. Take the buttons out of the oven and let them cool. Then paint a layer of varnish on the front of each button. When they are dry, varnish the backs.

6. Fold a piece of cardboard in half. Sew the frog buttons onto the card and draw a picture, such as lily pads, around them with felt tip pens.

PASTA PRESENTS

Brightly painted pasta shapes can be turned into magnificent jewelry very easily. They also make pretty decorations around photograph frames or on a mirror. Try making this pasta bow jewelry box and filling it with pasta jewels.

Things you need

Different pasta shapes — bows, spirals, shells, wheels, or animals
Cardboard box
Poster paints (including gold)
Paintbrushes
Clear varnish or nail polish
Thin ribbon or rolled elastic
Scissors and strong glue

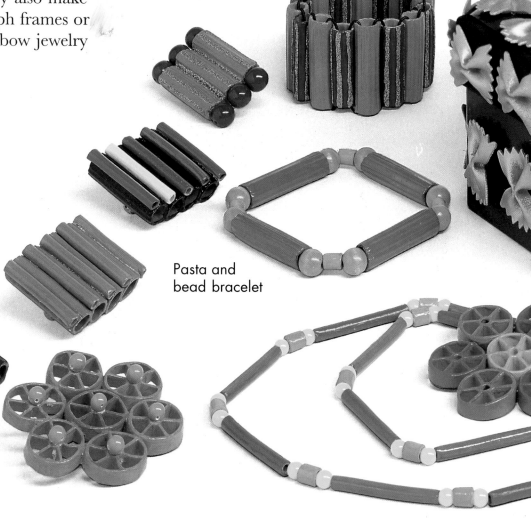

Pasta and
bead bracelet

Perfect pasta
brooches

Pasta bow box

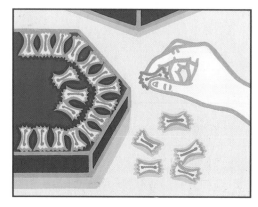

1. Before you start gluing, arrange the pasta bows on the cardboard box to see how they will look and how many you need.

2. Spread glue over the box, a little at a time. Then stick the pasta bows onto the glue. Do this until you have covered the top and sides of the box.

3. When all the bows are stuck firmly onto the box, paint them with gold poster paint. When the paint is dry, paint the bows with clear varnish.

Pasta bow
jewelry box

HANDY HINTS

If you do not have a plain colored box, you can paint it before you start gluing on the pasta.

Always varnish your pasta jewelry after you have painted it. Otherwise it might get soggy if it gets wet or damp.

To make pasta jewelry look very rich, paint it with gold or silver paint, cover it with glue, and dip it in glitter. You can also use glitter glue.

Pretty
pasta tube
necklace

Pretty pasta necklace

1. Paint some long and short spiral pasta tubes with bright poster paints. It is best to paint the tubes half at a time and then let them dry.

2. When the paint is absolutely dry, carefully brush a thick layer of clear nail polish over each one of the pasta tubes. Let the polish dry completely.

3. Cut a piece of thin ribbon a little longer than you want the necklace to be. Thread the painted pasta onto the ribbon and tie the ends in a bow.

PAINTED PLATES

Painted plates make wonderful presents to hang on the wall! You can paint them with bright patterns or pictures, for Christmas, birthdays, or a new baby. It is best to use glazed china plates and special enamel or acrylic paints. You can find them in most craft and art supply stores.

Things you need

Paper, a pencil, and colored pens
White glazed china plate
China marker
Paintbrushes and turpentine
Enamel or acrylic paints in
  bright colors
Saucers to mix paints

Hang your funny feast plate in the kitchen.

Clown plate for a baby

Paint a pattern instead of a picture.

14

Funny feast

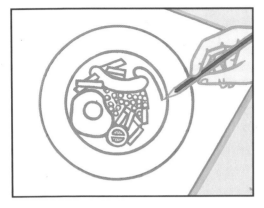

1. For practice, trace your plate on paper. Draw and color a fried egg, two sausages, a tomato, french fries, and peas, as shown.

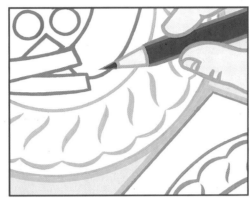

2. Turn the picture around to make sure it looks good from all angles. Copy the design onto a plain glazed plate, using a china marker.

3. If you are using enamel paints, stir them well before you begin to paint. Do not mix colors. Start by painting in a background color, as shown.

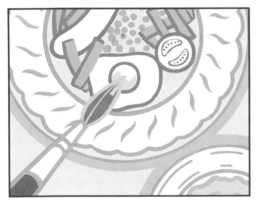

4. When the background color is completely dry, paint in the rest of your design. Do not put too much paint on the brush, but gradually build up the color.

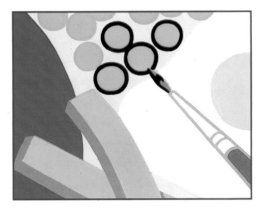

5. When you have finished painting, put the plate on newspaper to dry completely. Using a thin brush, add a black outline to the picture.

6. You will have to be very careful and keep a steady hand when you outline your picture. You can outline it in any color or not at all if you prefer.

HANDY HINTS

Read the instructions carefully before you use your paints as different brands of enamel paint dry in different ways.

Never eat off your painted plates or put them in the dishwasher as the hot water may make them peel. Wash them with dish-washing liquid.

Make sure you have lots of turpentine for washing your brushes and thinning your paint. You can wipe off your mistakes with a soft cloth dipped in turpentine.

Try using acrylic paints. They are not as shiny as enamels, but they dry more quickly.

FABULOUS FRAMES

Everybody loves being given photographs of their family, friends, or pets, especially if they are nicely framed. Try making these fabulous frames out of cardboard decorated with metal or tinfoil. You can also make shiny foil Christmas decorations and candleholders.

Things you need

Paper, pencil, and ruler
Cardboard, scissors, and masking tape
Metal foil from an empty tomato
  paste tube, or tinfoil cut from a
  clean foil baking tray
Photograph
Ballpoint pen
Strong glue or glue stick

Tomato paste
tube frame

Shiny Christmas
tree decorations

Tinfoil frame

16

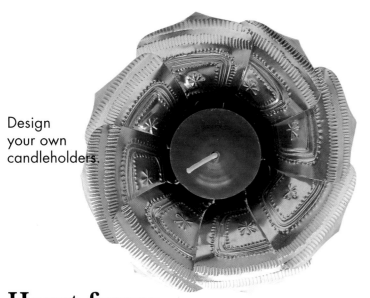

Design
your own
candleholders.

Heart frame

1. Cut the lid off an empty tomato paste tube with scissors. Cut the tube open and wash it out. Flatten it with your hand — be careful of sharp edges. Let the foil dry.

2. Draw a heart shape, about 5 in. high, on cardboard. It should be no bigger than your piece of foil. Draw a rectangle, about 4 in. long and 1 in. wide. Cut out both cardboard shapes.

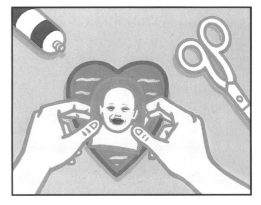

3. Cut out the photograph you want to frame and glue it to the middle of the cardboard heart, as shown. It is probably best to cut out just the face so it will show through the frame.

4. Using the tips of your scissors, score a line across the rectangular cardboard shape, about 1 in. from one end. Fold it over and tape it to the back of the heart shape with masking tape.

5. Trace the cardboard heart shape onto the written side of the metal foil with a ballpoint pen. Cut it out. Draw a smaller heart in the middle of the foil, as shown, and cut it out.

6. Using a ballpoint pen, draw patterns on the back of the foil heart. Press hard. Stick the heart, shiny side up, onto the cardboard heart, with the photograph showing through.

MERRY MOBILES

Colorful mobiles make great presents for babies because they love to look at interesting things that move about. Try choosing a theme, such as animals, monsters, or these birds, when you are designing your mobile. Use bright colors and simple shapes.

Things you need

Paper and pencil
10 squares of felt in
   bright colors
Needle and strong thread
Fabric glue
Scissors and pins
Lampshade ring or
   wooden embroidery ring
Colored thread
   or yarn

Make the birds as colorful as possible.

Bright bird mobile

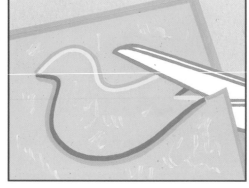

1. Draw a simple bird shape, as shown, on thin cardboard. Cut it out. Put the shape on a felt square and draw around it. Cut out a felt bird.

2. Glue the felt bird onto a felt square and cut around it so you have a double-thick felt bird. Make ten birds out of different-colored felt.

3. Now draw a wing shape, as shown, on thin cardboard. Cut it out. Put it on felt and cut around it. Cut out ten pairs of wings in different colors.

HANDY HINTS

You can make the felt animals with or without stuffing in the middle. The stuffing makes them a little bit thicker and stiffer.

Instead of gluing the felt shapes together, try sewing them together with bright thread.

Look in picture books to get ideas for your mobile and for simple shapes to copy.

Magic moons and stars mobile

Monster mobile

4. Glue a wing onto each side of every felt bird. Then cut 20 eyes and 20 beaks out of the felt. Glue them onto both sides of each bird. Let the glue dry.

5. Sew a long piece of colored thread with a knot in one end to the middle of each bird, as shown. Tie the birds at different lengths around the lampshade ring.

6. Tie three pieces of thread, about 1 ft. long, around the ring. Knot the ends together. Hang up the mobile and move the birds until it balances.

BRILLIANT BEADS

On these two pages you can find out how to make all sorts of beads from self-hardening clay. Most craft and art supply stores sell it in bright colors. You can mix colors together to make exciting and interesting patterns. Try making your own designs and shapes.

Things you need

Self-hardening clay in bright colors
Toothpick
Thin colored string or ribbon

Flower and bead necklace

Big bright necklace

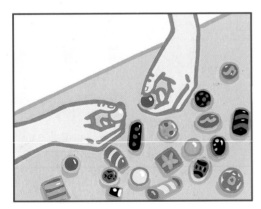

1. Choose the big bright beads you want to make, or design beads of your own. Try making them in lots of different shapes, sizes, colors and patterns.

2. Push a toothpick through each bead so you can thread it. Put the beads on a baking tray. Bake according to the instructions on the package.

3. When the beads are cool, decide which ones you want to put next to each other to make a necklace or bracelet. Thread the beads on colored string.

HANDY HINTS

It's easier to mold self-hardening clay once you have softened it in your hands. Roll it out on a clean surface to keep it from getting dirty, and keep the colors separate.

It helps to draw the design of your beads on paper before you start to make them, and to choose which colors you want to use.

You can varnish your beads once they are baked to make them brighter and shiny.

Roll out long, thin strips of clay to decorate different shapes, like these fish and wheels.

Big bright beads

To make this bead, roll out very thin strips of clay and make tiny balls. Press them on to a square bead to make a face.

To make a flower, flatten a small ball of clay. Cut out six wedges with a knife. Then mold the petals with your fingers.

To make a striped bead, make two separate beads in different colors. Slice the beads and then put them together, first one color and then the other. Roll until it is smooth.

To make this flower, press five little triangles of clay onto a flat bead in a flower shape. Then very carefully flatten the flower with a rolling pin. Add the center and the stripes.

To make a marbled bead, mix two colors together in a ball. Roll the ball until it is completely smooth.

To make a bead with swirls flatten two small balls of different colors. Roll them together like a jelly roll. Cut off thin slices, press them on a big bead, and roll until smoothed.

FUNNY FAMILY FIGURINES

For an original present, try making funny figurines of your family and friends — even your pets! You can make them out of salt dough (see page 6 for the recipe). The figurines look even funnier if you give each person a special feature that reminds you especially of them.

Things you need

Salt dough (see page 6)
Tempera or poster paints
Paintbrushes
Clear varnish or nail polish
Garlic press
Toothpick
Pencil
Baking tray

Make an angel Christmas decoration.

Make a nice fat Santa Claus.

Figurine of Mom

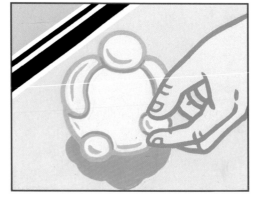

1. Draw a picture of the person you want to make, or use a photograph. The figurine must have a solid body, as shown, to stand on when it is baked.

2. Roll a big ball of dough for the body and press it onto a baking tray. Press on a smaller ball for the head. Make sausage-shaped arms and round feet.

3. When you have made the body, add the features. Push balls of dough through a garlic press for the hair. Press on a nose and mouth.

Family of salt dough figurines

HANDY HINTS

Salt dough figurines take different lengths of time to harden in the oven depending on how big and fat they are. It is best to check them while they are cooking. Small figures take about 30 to 40 minutes.

Knead the dough well before you use it. The softer it is, the easier it is to use.

It's best to make your models short and fat rather than tall, as they spread out when they are baking.

4. Use a toothpick to poke holes for the eyes and to make finger lines. Add something special that reminds you of the person, such as a particular dress or tie.

5. Let the figurine dry out a little. Then put it in the oven at 350°F until it is hard. Take it out and let it cool. Paint it with bright poster or tempera paints.

6. When the paint is dry, varnish the figurine all over and let dry. Then brush another coat of varnish onto the front and back. Let dry.

MARVELOUS MAGNETS

These nifty magnets are easy and fun to make and are super presents for people of all ages. They stick on any metal surface, such as a refrigerator or a filing cabinet, and are useful for holding up notes, lists, and pictures.

Things you need

Candies, such as brightly colored jelly beans or lollipops
Small, round magnets (available from hardware stores)
Mini baking cups and strong glue
Clear varnish and paintbrush

Small bright objects make the best and prettiest magnets. You will probably be able to find lots of good objects to use around the house. Most things just need a magnet stuck on the back, but some may need to be varnished.

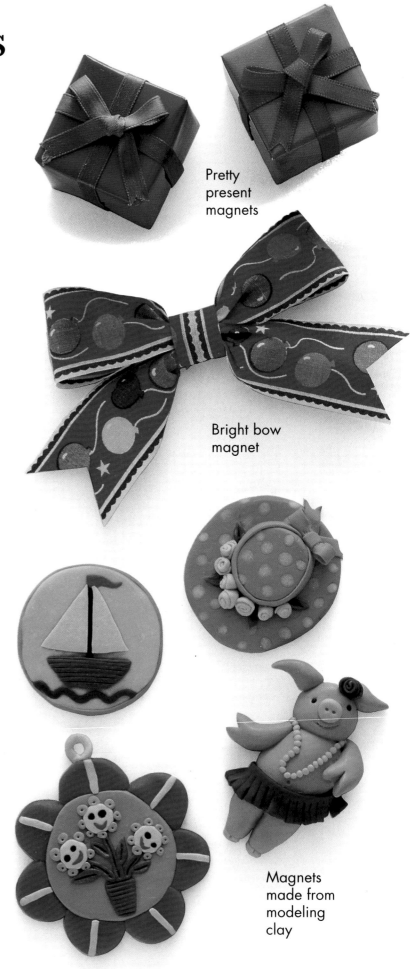

Pretty present magnets

Bright bow magnet

Magnets made from modeling clay

HANDY HINTS

Allow lots of time for the coats of varnish to dry on your magnets. Start making them a few days before you want to give them away as presents.

If you are using cookies or candies, it is best to let them dry out before you varnish them.

Before you start, varnish a candy to test the color.

Varnished jam tart magnet

Use many different kinds of candy.

Painted, varnished cookie magnets

A basketful of flowers

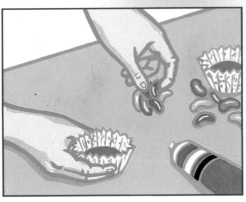

Jelly bean magnet

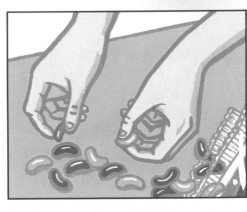

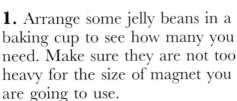

1. Arrange some jelly beans in a baking cup to see how many you need. Make sure they are not too heavy for the size of magnet you are going to use.

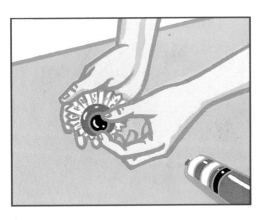

2. Glue the jelly beans together with strong glue and let them dry. Stick them into two mini baking cups, one inside the other. Let the glue dry.

3. Cover completely with clear varnish. Let dry and then varnish again three or four times. Make sure the varnish dries between each coat.

4. As soon as the varnish is dry and hard, stick a magnet onto the bottom of the mini baking cup. Let it dry. Now try making other kinds of magnets.

FELT PICTURES

These fantastic felt pictures make perfect presents for moms, dads, and grandparents. They are made out of pieces of colored felt stuck or sewn on top of each other. They can also be decorated with buttons, beads, and bright embroidery thread. If you don't have any felt, you can use another kind of fabric instead.

Things you need

Drawing paper
Tracing paper
Pencil and eraser
Scissors
Fabric glue
Squares of felt in different colors
Sewing pins

My dad

Cool cat picture

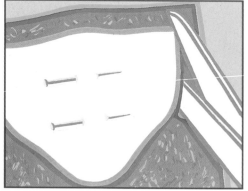

1. On a sheet of paper, draw the picture you are going to make in the same size as you want it to be. Start with something simple, such as this cool cat.

2. Trace the cat's face onto tracing paper and cut it out. Use this as a paper pattern. Pin the paper pattern onto a square of felt and cut around it.

3. Now trace the cat's hat, bow tie, shirt, and coat. Cut them out separately. Pin each paper pattern onto a different felt square and cut them out.

Cool cat

My house

4. Using fabric glue, stick the felt cat's face onto a big square of felt of a different color. Then glue on the hat, bow tie, shirt, and coat, as shown. Let the glue dry.

5. Cut out and glue some long whiskers on the cat's cheeks. Trace and cut out sunglasses and glue them on the cat's face. Glue a band on the hat.

6. Cut out small pieces of felt for the nose, mouth, and ears and glue them on. Add different-colored lapels and a pocket handkerchief to the coat.

27

BEAUTIFUL BOWS

These beautiful bows are very easy to make with just newspaper, glue, and paint. They can be made into brooches and earrings, or turned into colorful cuff links. Decorated with poster paints and then varnished, they can be stuck onto hair bands, hair combs, or shoes.

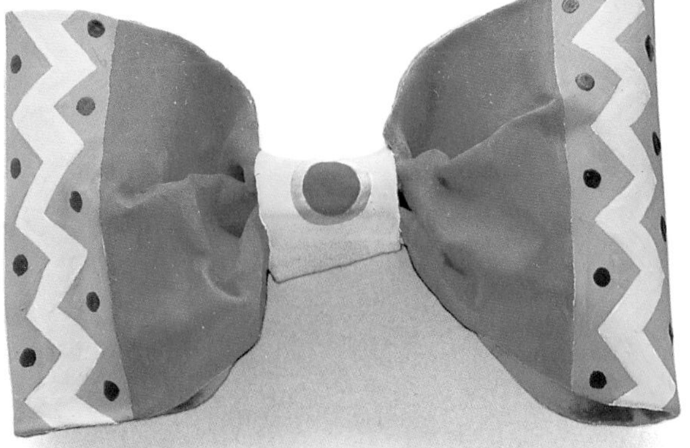

Things you need

Newspaper
Wallpaper paste
Bowl of water
Tempera or poster paints and
    paintbrush
Clear gloss varnish
    or nail polish
Strong glue (for sticking
    on brooch backs,
    earrings, cuff links, or
    hair combs)
Brooch back

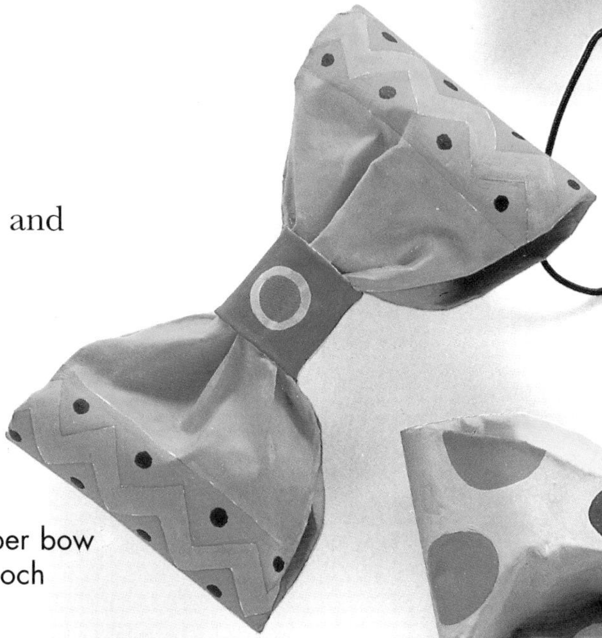

Paper bow
brooch

Polka-dot
paper
bow tie

Beautiful bow
hair combs

Pretty
paper bow
brooch

28

Snappy
shoe bows

Paper bow brooch

1. Mix the wallpaper paste following the instructions on the package. Then rip large sheets of newspaper into quarters and soak them, one by one, in cold water, for a few seconds.

2. Take the paper out of the water and lay it flat on a table. Peel off the top strip and spread paste over it with your hands or a paintbrush. Carefully rip the glued paper in half lengthways.

3. Stick one half of the paper to the other so that an unglued side sticks to a glued one. Do this again so you have a long strip of paper four layers deep. Cut off a strip at one end.

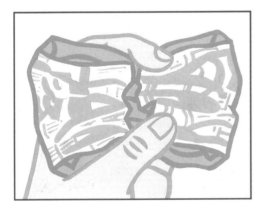

4. Fold in the edges of the long strip to neaten them. Then fold the two ends into the middle to make a bow shape, as shown. Pinch the middle to make the bow look nice and full.

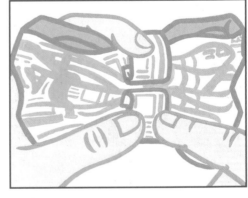

5. Now fold in the edges of the little strip to neaten them. Wrap the strip around the bow so that it covers the join in the middle. Fold the ends under and leave the bow to dry.

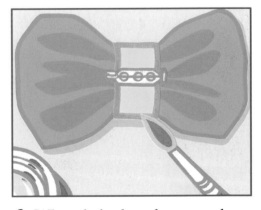

6. When it is dry, decorate the bow with poster paint. Let it dry and then paint on a pattern. Stick the bow onto a brooch back with strong glue. Then varnish it to make it look shiny.

PICTURE PRESENTS

Old boxes and tin cans can be made to look beautiful by decorating them with lots of tiny pictures or patterns cut out from postcards, glossy magazines, birthday cards, or wrapping paper, and then varnished. You can also try decorating hairbrushes, hand mirrors, and photograph frames with cut-out pictures.

Things you need

Box or tin can
Old magazines, wrapping paper,
  birthday cards, or postcards
Small scissors
Strong glue or glue stick
Clear varnish
Fine sandpaper
Paintbrush
Soft cloth

Make a frame to cover with pictures.

Picture box

Cover a box for Dad with old stamps and varnish.

Choose a simple picture to stick on a hairbrush.

Pretty picture box

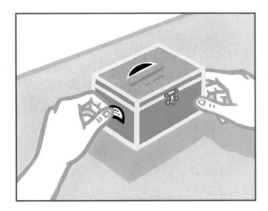

1. Before you start, make sure that the box or tin can is clean and smooth so that it is ready to decorate. Peel off any labels or bumpy bits.

2. Using a pair of small, sharp scissors, carefully cut out the pictures you want to cover the box with. To start with, practice cutting out bigger pictures.

3. Arrange the pictures on the box and then glue on the first one. Rub hard to get rid of any air bubbles and to make a smooth surface.

4. Wipe off extra glue with a soft cloth and glue on the next picture. Continue until you have covered the box with little pictures. Let the glue dry.

5. Once the glue has dried you can begin to varnish. Brush on the first coat and let it dry overnight. Then gently sand it down with fine sandpaper.

6. Dust the box and then varnish on another coat. Let each coat dry before adding the next. You will need ten layers of varnish. Do not sand the last coat.

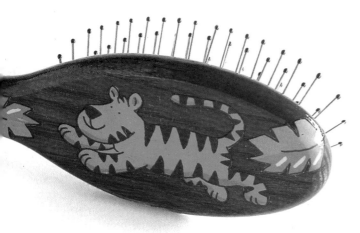

HANDY HINTS

It's best to use good quality pictures to decorate presents. Save wrapping paper, postcards, and Christmas and birthday cards.

Before you start, decide what kinds of pictures you are going to use, such as birds or flowers. You can also use old stamps and even shells, buttons, sequins, or beads.

GLORIOUS GLOVES

Here's a really different kind of present to give to someone to make them laugh. You can buy cheap dish-washing gloves and cotton gloves in many bright colors from hardware or grocery stores to make these crazy gloves.

Things you need
for dish-washing gloves

Two pairs of rubber gloves
  in different colors
Plastic shopping bag
Needle, thread, and pins
Strong glue
Scissors and pencil

for dust glove

Cotton glove
Dust rag or cloth
Felt for the nails
Diamantés and sequins
Fabric glue or needle
  and thread

Cut circles out of balloons to decorate the gloves.

Wild dish-washing gloves

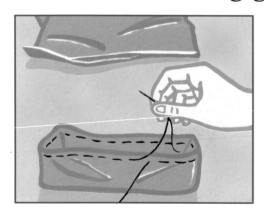

1. Cut a strip, about 3 in. wide and 15 in. long, out of a plastic bag. Thread a needle and sew a running stitch as close to one edge as possible, as shown.

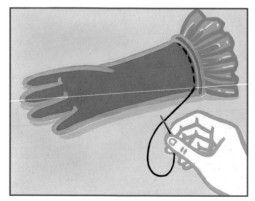

2. Take out the needle and pull up the thread to make a frilly cuff. When it is small enough to fit around a rubber glove, pin it and sew it on, as shown.

3. Repeat with the other glove of the same color. Then cut out ten fingernails and flowers from the different-colored glove. Stick them on the gloves with glue.

Dainty dust
glove

Grisly
gardening
gloves

HANDY HINTS

Before you start decorating your dish-washing gloves, test the glue to make sure it sticks.

Be careful not to stick or sew the front of the glove to the back when you are putting the dust rag on the dusting glove.

Try sticking diamanté shapes onto the dish-washing gloves to make them look fancy.

Dainty dust glove

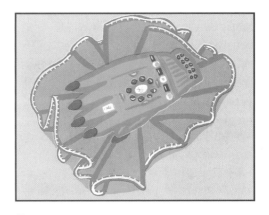

1. Draw five fingernails on the felt. Make sure they are big enough to fit on the ends of the fingers of the cotton glove. Cut them out.

2. Using fabric glue, stick one felt nail onto the tip of each finger of the cotton glove, as shown. Let the glue dry.

3. Carefully stick or sew the dust rag to the middle of the glove, as shown. Then stick or sew bright diamantés and sequins onto the glove to decorate it.

33

SWEET PRESENTS

When you do not have much time to make a present, why not give some delicious homemade candies? These are very quick to make, as you don't have to cook them. You can make them even more special by putting them in a pretty box or basket tied with a bow.

Things you need
for the marzipan fruits*

1 cup almond paste
1 whipped egg white
1½ cups powdered sugar
Lemon juice
Food coloring
Bowl, wooden spoon
  and fork

for coconut ice

2½ cups powdered sugar
1 teaspoon of vanilla extract
Small can of condensed milk
¼ cup shredded coconut
Red food coloring
2 bowls
Wooden spoon
Baking pan and knife

Fill a tiny basket with all kinds of marzipan fruits.

Put the coconut ice in mini baking cups in a box.

34   *Ready-made marzipan may be used if salmonella poisoning is a concern.

Marzipan fruits

1. Gradually add almond paste to whipped egg white. Add powdered sugar. If the mixture is too dry, add lemon juice, a little at a time, until you have a soft ball of marzipan.

2. Divide the marzipan into four separate lumps. Put each lump into a bowl. Then add a few drops of a different color food coloring to each bowl. Mix it well with a fork.

3. Shape the marzipan mixture into fruits — red for strawberries and plums, yellow for bananas and lemons, green for apples and pears. Use cloves for stalks and green marzipan to make leaves.

Make lines on the bananas.

Dip the strawberries in sugar.

Roll the oranges around the outside of a fine grater.

Coconut ice

1. Sift the sugar into a bowl and then add the vanilla extract and condensed milk. Add the shredded coconut and stir the mixture with a wooden spoon until it becomes stiff.

2. Divide the mixture in half and put one half in the second bowl. Add a few drops of red food coloring to one of the mixtures and stir it until it becomes pale pink.

3. Put the white mixture in the bottom of the baking pan. Put it in the refrigerator until firm. Spread the pink mixture on top and put it in the refrigerator. When it is hard, cut into squares.

35

GREAT GINGERBREAD PRESENTS

Gingerbread is simple to make and delicious to eat. You can make it into almost any shape you like, such as gingerbread people and animals, a gingerbread house, decorations to hang on a Christmas tree, and even name plates for your friends and family.

Things you need

1¼ cups self-rising flour
1 tablespoon ground ginger
6 tablespoons butter
¼ cup corn syrup
½ cup soft brown sugar
3 tablespoons milk
Margarine or oil (for greasing
  baking tray)
Flour (for flouring work top)
Tube of ready-made icing
Sifter, large bowl, and
  a wooden spoon
Rolling pin and baking tray
Cookie cutters in different
  shapes and sizes
Toothpick

Gingerbread family

Making the gingerbread

1. Preheat oven to 325°F. Sift the flour and ginger together into the bowl. Then, using your fingertips, rub the butter into the mixture.

2. Mix the syrup, sugar, and milk together and add them to the flour mixture. Mix them into a dough. Put the dough in the refrigerator for an hour.

3. Grease the baking tray with oil or margarine. Lightly flour the work space and roll out the dough with a rolling pin to a thickness of about ¼ in.

HANDY HINTS

If you do not have cookie cutters, use cardboard shapes and cut around them.

To keep syrup off a spoon, rub the spoon with butter, dip it in flour, and then put the spoon in the syrup.

Gingerbread Christmas decorations

Gingerbread name plates

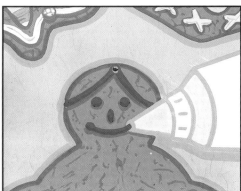

Gingerbread animals

4. Using cookie cutters, cut out some gingerbread cookies. Put them on the baking tray, leaving gaps between the shapes to allow them to spread.

5. Make a small hole near the top of each shape with a toothpick. Bake cookies in the oven for 10 to 15 minutes, or until they are golden brown.

6. When the gingerbread cookies are cool, draw faces, names, or patterns on them with the icing. Thread ribbon through the holes before you give them away.

PAPER BOWLS

These colorful bowls are made out of papier-mâché. They make wonderful fruit bowls, pencil and pen holders, or special vases for flowers. You can paint your own designs on them or decorate them with colored sugar or tissue paper.

Things you need

Large bowl (to use as a mold)
Plastic wrap or petroleum jelly
Newspaper
Wallpaper paste
Bowl for mixing glue
Paintbrush and water
Tempera or poster paints
Scissors
Clear varnish

Papier-mâché a jam jar to make a waterproof vase. Keep the jar in place for the water.

Perfect paper bowl

Perfect paper bowl

1. Cover the outside of the bowl you are using as a mold with plastic wrap. Make sure that the plastic wrap covers the edge of the bowl. This will stop the papier-mâché from sticking to the edge.

2. Mix the wallpaper paste, following the instructions on the package.

3. Tear the newspaper into big pieces. Drop them, one by one, into 3 in. of water in a sink. Wet them for five minutes and then carefully take them out. Lay them down on a work surface.

HANDY HINTS

Instead of using plastic wrap, you can use petroleum jelly to stop the papier-mâché from sticking to the bowl.

If the papier-mâché shell tears when you take it off the bowl, fix it with masking tape. Papier-mâché over the tear.

To make a pencil holder, papier-mâché an old salt canister or box. Separate it from the plastic wrap with a dinner knife.

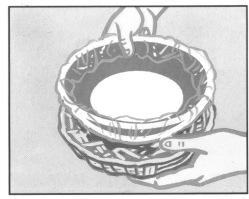

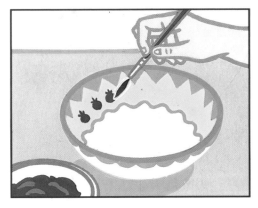

4. Tear the wet newspaper into small strips. Cover the outside of the bowl with a layer of strips. Make sure that they overlap so that they cover the plastic wrap. Brush the paste over the strips.

5. Cover the paste with more strips. Let it dry. Add more paste and paper until you have five or six layers of papier-mâché. When it is dry, separate the paper and paste shell from the bowl.

6. Trim the edges with scissors. Paint the bowl all over with tempera or poster paints. When it is dry, paint on bright patterns. To give it a glossy look, brush on a layer of clear varnish.

COLORFUL CANDLEHOLDERS

For special occasions, such as Christmas, birthday parties, or even spooky Halloween parties, it is fun to have candles burning on the table. Try making these colorful salt dough candleholders to help decorate the table.

Things you need

Ready-made salt dough (see page 6)
Rolling pin, knife, and baking tray
Round cookie cutters or a glass
Thin cardboard and scissors
Tempera or poster paints and
  paintbrush
Clear varnish or nail polish
Strong glue and Plasticine
Two thin candles

Slithery snake
candleholder

Deep
candleholder
filled with
candies

Holder for thick
candles

Christmas
candleholder

Spooky
Halloween
holder

Christmas candleholders

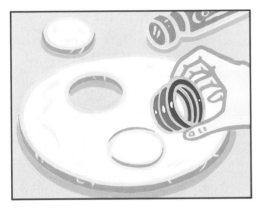

1. Turn the oven on to 350°F. Roll out the dough until it is about ½ in. thick. Cut out two circles of dough with a round cookie cutter or a glass.

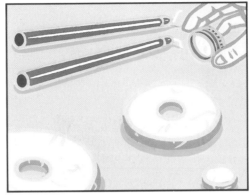

2. Cut out a circle in the middle of the round shapes of dough a little bigger than the end of a candle. Use a small round cookie cutter or a bottle top.

3. Cut out salt dough holly leaves and roll small balls to make the berries. Stick them around the circle of dough with water, as shown.

4. Put the Christmas rings in the oven on a baking tray until they are hard. This should take about an hour. Take them out and let them cool completely.

5. When they are cool, put the rings on a piece of cardboard and draw around them. Cut out the circles. Glue them to the bottom of the rings, as shown.

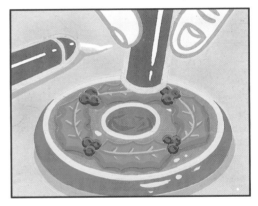

6. Paint the candleholders with poster paints. When the paint is dry, brush on a layer of varnish. Stick Plasticine in the holes and press in the candles.

HANDY HINTS

Let the salt dough candleholders dry out a little before you bake them in the oven.

Instead of using cookie cutters, you can cut out the dough rings with jar lids or ramekin dishes.

You can make little bowls for your candles by covering an upturned ramekin dish with salt dough and baking it in the oven. Be very careful not to break the salt dough shell when you take it off the ramekin dish.

POTTED PLANT STICKS

For an unusual present, especially for people who love flowers and gardening, you can make these potted plant sticks. They are very useful for propping up flowers in a potted plant and they help drain the water through the soil.

Things you need

Thin wooden sticks about 8 in. long
  (thin dowels or garden markers
  are best)
Scraps of colored felt
Self-hardening clay in bright colors
Fabric glue and baking tray
Pencil and paper

Spooky
glow-in-the-dark
skull stick

Felt flower
plant sticks

Modeling
clay fish
stick

Two-faced
pig stick

Use glow-in-the-
dark modeling
clay to make this
spooky spider.

42

HANDY HINTS

Use old lollipop sticks to make plant sticks for tiny pots. They also make good table decorations for parties.

Try making some spooky plant sticks with special glow-in-the-dark clay or paint.

Salt dough (see page 6), papier-mâché animals, flowers, bows, and thick painted cardboard shapes make good potted plant sticks.

Felt flower plant stick

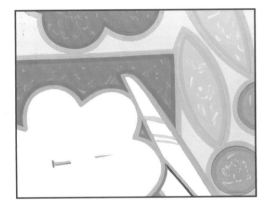 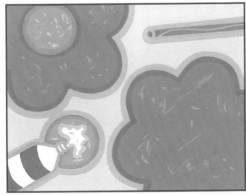 

1. Draw a flower on paper and cut it out. Pin the shape on felt and cut around it. Do this again. Cut out two felt leaves and two flower centers.

2. Spread glue on one side of each flower center and stick them onto the middle of the flower shapes, as shown. Leave the glue to dry completely.

3. Glue the flowers together, as shown, with the top of the stick sandwiched between them. Glue the leaves together with the stick between one end.

Two-faced pig stick

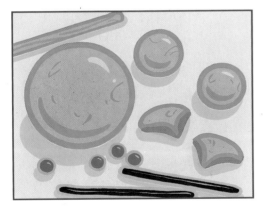 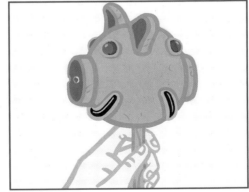 

1. Roll a ball of bright pink self-hardening clay for the pig's head and two smaller balls for its noses. Make four little blue eyes, two pink ears, and two black mouths.

2. Press a nose, two eyes, and a mouth onto each side of the head. Put on the ears. Push a stick into the head where the neck would be, about 1 in. deep.

3. Take the stick out and bake the pig's head in the oven according to the instructions on the package. Before the clay cools, push the stick back into the hole.

CRAZY STRING HOLDERS

Turn your empty yogurt containers or plastic tubs into these crazy animal heads. Fixed to the wall, they make great holders for string, ribbon, and yarn. You can use all sorts of different shaped and sized pots, which you can probably find around the house.

Things you need

Empty plastic containers
Thin cardboard (an old cereal
   box is ideal)
Acrylic paints and paintbrush
Pencil
Scissors and thumbtacks
Small balls of string, ribbon,
   or yarn
Strong glue or glue stick
Beads

Striped tiger
string holder

Striped tiger holder

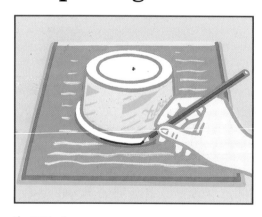

1. Wash out an empty yogurt container. Soak it in water and peel off any labels. When it is dry, trace the container onto some thin cardboard, as shown.

2. For the striped tiger, add big round ears. Carefully cut around them and the cardboard shape. Then cut a flap, as shown, in the middle of the cardboard shape.

3. Cover the container with a thick layer of white acrylic paint. Let it dry. Then paint on a layer of orange paint and let it dry. Paint on the stripes, as shown.

Big bull holder

HANDY HINTS

Do not put a big ball of string or yarn into your crazy string holder as it may be too heavy and will pull the holder off the wall.

You can put all sorts of things onto your string heads to make them look even crazier. Use cotton balls for sheep, yarn for a horse's mane, buttons for noses, and beads for eyes.

Happy pig holder

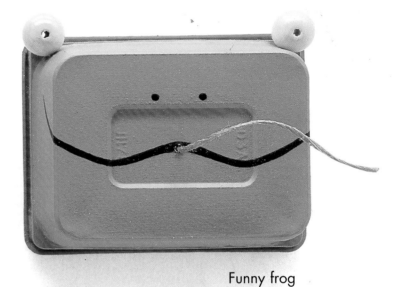

Funny frog holder

4. When the paint is dry, paint on the tiger's nose and mouth. Make sure the mouth is where you want the string to come out. Glue on some string whiskers.

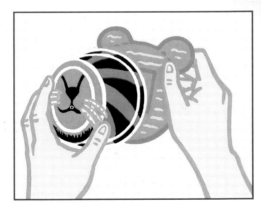

5. Using small scissors, poke a hole in the mouth. Then glue the cardboard shape onto the back of the container. Paint the tiger's ears orange and black.

6. Glue on bead eyes. Put some string into the container. Pull one end through the mouth. To stick the holder on the wall, push a thumbtack through each ear.

WRAPPING IT UP

Now that you have made your presents, it's very important to know how to wrap them up properly to make them look super special. Here are some wonderful wrapping ideas and ways to decorate your presents with bows and paper ribbons. Instead of buying paper you could try to make your own.

Things you need

Wrapping paper
Clear tape
Scissors
Thin paper ribbon
Sheets of paper in
   different colors

Use a potato or stencil to print patterns on homemade wrapping paper.

You can make long, tricky-shaped presents look like real crackers. Tie bows around the ends.

Perfect present

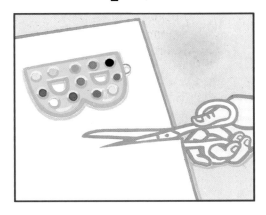

1. Put the present on a sheet of wrapping paper to see how much you need. Make sure you have enough to fold in both ends and to overlap the paper at the top. Cut the paper.

2. Put the present facedown on the paper. Fold the long edges over the top so that they overlap. Make sure the paper is tight before you tape it.

3. Turn one end of the present toward you and fold in the ends as neatly as possible to make corner folds, as shown. Tape them down. Do the same to the other end of the paper.

Curls and bows

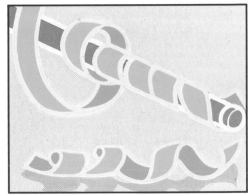

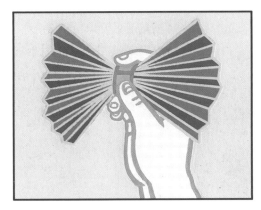

1. Decorate your present with curly paper ribbon. To make the ribbon curl, hold it between your thumb and the blade of a pair of scissors. Firmly pull the blade along the ribbon.

2. You can make your own paper curls by cutting out strips of paper and wrapping them around a wooden spoon or stick. Try using different widths and colors.

3. Make a pleated paper bow by folding some paper over and over again like an accordion. Pinch the middle and wrap a strip of paper around it. Tape or glue it.

Make gift tags out of colored paper. Tie them on with thin ribbon.

HANDY HINTS

To make your packages look best, fold in the sides and ends of your paper before you start to wrap.

If you don't have any wrapping paper you can use newspaper comics or tinfoil. Decorating plain paper with potato prints or stencils is also nice.